CONTENTS

God Has Promised

For any gift He has promised, we may ask; then we are to believe that we receive, and return thanks to God that we have received.—*Education*, p. 258.

God stands back of every promise He has made.—*Christ's Object Lessons*, p. 147.

Can you not trust in your heavenly Father? Can you not rest upon His gracious promise? . . . Can we not have implicit trust, knowing that He is faithful who hath promised? I entreat you to let your trembling faith again grasp the promises of God. Bear your whole weight upon them with unwavering faith; for they will not, they cannot, fail.—*Testimonies*, vol. 2, p. 497.

Let these blessed promises, set in the framework of faith, be placed in memory's halls. Not one of them will fail. All that God hath spoken He will do. "He is faithful that promised."—*Ibid.*, vol. 5, p. 630.

We should now acquaint ourselves with God by proving His promises. Angels record every prayer that is earnest and sincere. We should rather dispense with selfish gratifications than neglect communion with God.—*The Great Controversy*, p. 622.

Our heavenly Father has a thousand ways to provide for us, of which we know nothing.—*The Desire of Ages*, p. 330.

Think of Christ. Look to Him in faith, believing His promises. Keep your mind trustful. He will be your stay. Lean on Him, depend on Him. . . . Put your trust in One whose arm will never fail. . . . Looking to Jesus you will find encouragement.—*Selected Messages*, book 2, p. 265.

The Comforter that Christ promised to send in His name abides with us. In the way that leads to the City of God there are no difficulties which those who trust in Him may not overcome. There are no dangers which they may not escape. There is not a sorrow, not a grievance, not a human weakness, for which He has not provided a remedy.—*The Ministry of Healing*, p. 249.

All things are possible to him that believeth; and whatsoever things we desire when we pray, if we believe that we receive them we shall have them. This faith will penetrate the darkest cloud and bring rays of light and hope to the drooping, desponding soul. It is the absence of this faith and trust which brings perplexity, distressing fears, and surmisings of evil. God will do great things for His people when they put their entire trust in Him.—*Testimonies*, vol. 2, p. 140.

All His [God's] gifts are promised on condition of obedience.—*Christ's Object Lessons*, p. 145.

The enemy never can take out of the hand of Christ the one who is simply trusting in His promises.—*The SDA Bible Commentary*, Ellen G. White Comments, on Rev. 3:3, p. 959.

If you have . . . given yourself to Christ you

are a member of the family of God, and everything in the Father's house is for you. All the treasures of God are opened to you, both the world that now is and that which is to come. The ministry of angels, the gift of His Spirit, the labors of His servants—all are for you. The world, with everything in it, is yours so far as it can do you good. Even the enmity of the wicked will prove a blessing by disciplining you for heaven. If "ye are Christ's," "all things are yours."—*Thoughts From the Mount of Blessing*, p. 110.

To him who is content to receive without deserving, who feels that he can never recompense such love, who lays all doubt and unbeliefs aside, and comes as a little child to the feet of Jesus, all the treasures of eternal love are a free, everlasting gift.—Ellen G. White letter 19E, 1892.

It is through the gift of Christ that we receive every blessing. Through that gift there comes to us day by day the unfailing flow of Jehovah's goodness. Every flower, with its delicate tints and sweet fragrance, is given for our enjoyment through that one Gift. The sun and moon were made by Him; there is not a star that beautifies

10

the heavens which He did not make. There is not an article of food upon our tables that He has not provided for our sustenance. The superscription of Christ is upon it all.—*Testimonies,* vol. 8, pp. 287, 288.

The Saviour has not promised His followers the luxuries of the world; their fare may be plain, and even scanty; their lot may be shut in by poverty; but His word is pledged that their need shall be supplied, and He has promised that which is far better than worldly good—the abiding comfort of His presence.—*The Desire of Ages,* p. 367.

He [Christ] is to be with us, not only at the beginning and the end of our course, but at every step of the way.—*Steps to Christ,* p. 69.

It is possible even for a parent to turn away from his hungry child, but God can never reject the cry of the needy and longing heart.—*Thoughts From the Mount of Blessing,* p. 132.

Do You Need Strength?

God does not ask us to do in our own strength the work before us. He has provided divine assistance for all the emergencies to which our human resources are unequal.— *Testimonies*, vol. 8, p. 19.

When you rise in the morning, do you feel your helplessness and your need of strength from God? And do you humbly, heartily make known your wants to your heavenly Father? If so, angels mark your prayers, and if these prayers have not gone forth out of feigned lips, when you are in danger of unconsciously doing wrong and exerting an influence which will lead others to do wrong, your guardian angel will be by your side, prompting you to a better course, choosing your words for you, and influencing your actions.—*Ibid.*, vol. 3, pp. 363, 364.

Words cannot describe the peace and joy possessed by him who takes God at His word. Trials do not disturb him, slights do not vex him. Self is crucified. Day by day his duties may become more taxing, his temptations stronger, his trials more severe; but he does not falter; for he receives strength equal to his need.—*Messages to Young People*, p. 98.

In the darkest days, when appearances seem most forbidding, have faith in God. He is working out His will, doing all things well in behalf of His people. The strength of those who love and serve Him will be renewed day by day.—*The Ministry of Healing*, p. 482.

If we encounter difficulties, and in Christ's strength overcome them; if we meet enemies, and in Christ's strength put them to flight; if we accept responsibilities, and in Christ's strength discharge them faithfully, we are gaining a precious experience. We learn, as we could not otherwise have learned, that our Saviour is a present help in every time of need.—*Testimonies*, vol. 5, p. 34.

13

You can do nothing in your own strength, but in the strength of Jesus you can do all things.—*Ibid.*, vol. 4, p. 259.

The promises of God are full and abundant, and there is no need for anyone to depend upon humanity for strength. To all that call upon Him, God is near to help and succor.—*Testimonies to Ministers*, p. 381.

Strength and grace have been provided through Christ to be brought by ministering angels to every believing soul.—*Steps to Christ*, p. 53.

It is obstacles that make men strong. It is . . . difficulties, conflicts, rebuffs, that make men of moral sinew. Too much ease and avoiding responsibility have made weaklings and dwarfs of those who ought to be responsible men of moral power and strong spiritual muscle.—*Testimonies*, vol. 3, p. 495.

Are Your Burdens Too Great to Bear?

Through all trials we have a never-failing Helper. He does not leave us alone to struggle with temptation, to battle with evil, and be finally crushed with burdens and sorrow.—*The Desire of Ages*, p. 483.

Keep your wants, your joys, your sorrows, your cares, and your fears before God. You cannot burden Him; you cannot weary Him. He who numbers the hairs of your head is not indifferent to the wants of His children. "The Lord is very pitiful, and of tender mercy." His heart of love is touched by our sorrows and even by our utterances of them. Take to Him everything that perplexes the mind. Nothing is too great for Him to bear, for He holds up worlds, He rules over all the affairs of the universe. Nothing that in any way concerns our peace is too small for Him to notice. There is no chapter in our experience too dark for Him to read; there is no perplexity too difficult for Him to unravel. . . . No sincere prayer [can] escape the lips, of which our heavenly Father is unobservant, or in which He takes no immediate interest.—*Steps to Christ*, p. 100.

Whatever your anxieties and trials, spread out your case before the Lord. Your spirit will be braced for endurance. The way will be opened for you. . . . The weaker and more helpless you know yourself to be, the stronger will you become in His strength. The heavier your burdens, the more blessed the rest in casting them upon the Burden Bearer.—*The Desire of Ages*, p. 329.

It is true that disappointments will come; tribulations we must expect; but we are to commit everything, great and small, to God. He does not become perplexed by the multiplicity of our grievances nor overpowered by the weight of our burdens. His watchcare extends to every household and encircles every individual; He is concerned in all our business and our

16

sorrows. He marks every tear; He is touched with the feeling of our infirmities. All the afflictions and trials that befall us here are permitted, to work out His purposes of love toward us.—*Testimonies*, vol. 5, p. 742.

We need to trust in Jesus daily, hourly. He has promised that as our day is, our strength shall be. By His grace we may bear all the burdens of the present and perform its duties. But many are weighed down by the anticipation of future troubles. They are constantly seeking to bring tomorrow's burdens into today. Thus a large share of all their trials are imaginary. For these, Jesus has made no provision. He promises grace only for the day.—*Ibid.*, p. 200.

Do You Feel Sad?

All heaven is interested in the happiness of man. Our heavenly Father does not close the avenues of joy to any of His creatures.—*Steps to Christ*, p. 46.

Do not think that God wishes us to yield up everything which it is for our happiness here to retain. He requires us to give up only that which it would not be for our good and happiness to retain.—*Testimonies*, vol. 2, p. 588.

God would not have any of us remain pressed down by dumb sorrow, with sore and breaking hearts. . . . Oh, the blessed Saviour stands by many whose eyes are so blinded by tears that they do not discern Him. He longs to clasp our hands firmly, while we cling to Him in simple faith, imploring Him to guide us. . . . If we will let the comfort and peace of Jesus into our lives, we shall be kept close to His great heart of love.—*Selected Messages*, book 2, pp. 257, 258.

Many are sad and discouraged, weak in faith and trust. Let them do something to help someone more needy than themselves, and they will grow strong in God's strength.—*Christian Service*, p. 151.

Do not allow the perplexities and worries of everyday life to fret your mind and cloud your brow. If you do, you will always have something to vex and annoy. Life is what we make it, and we shall find what we look for. If we look for sadness and trouble, . . . we shall find plenty of them to engross our thoughts and our conversation. But if we look on the bright side of things, we shall find enough to make us cheerful and happy.—*The Adventist Home*, p. 430.

When the mind is free and happy from a sense of duty well done and the satisfaction of giving happiness to others, the cheering,

19

uplifting influence brings new life to the whole being.—*The Ministry of Healing*, p. 257.

Those who take Christ at His word, and surrender their souls to His keeping, their lives to His ordering, will find peace and quietude. Nothing of the world can make them sad when Jesus makes them glad by His presence.—*The Desire of Ages*, p. 331.

When the Spirit of God takes possession of the heart, it transforms the life. Sinful thoughts are put away, evil deeds are renounced; love, humility, and peace take the place of anger, envy, and strife. Joy takes the place of sadness, and the countenance reflects the light of heaven. No one sees the hand that lifts the burden, or beholds the light descend from the courts above. The blessing comes when by faith the soul surrenders itself to God.—*Ibid.*, p. 173.

It is the duty of God's children to be cheerful. They should encourage a happy frame of mind. God cannot be glorified by His children living continually under a cloud and casting a shadow wherever they go.—Ellen G. White, in *Review and Herald*, April 28, 1859.

Are You Discouraged?

It is Satan's work to discourage the soul; it is Christ's work to inspire with faith and hope.—*The Desire of Ages*, p. 249.

Satan is ready to steal away the blessed assurances of God. He desires to take every glimmer of hope and every ray of light from the soul; but you must not permit him to do this. Exercise faith; fight the good fight of faith; wrestle with these doubts; become acquainted with the promises.—*Testimonies*, vol. 5, p. 629.

Christian life is more than many take it to be. It does not consist wholly in gentleness, patience, meekness, and kindliness. These graces are essential; but there is need also of courage, force, energy, and perseverance. The path that Christ marks out is a narrow, self-denying path. To enter that path and press on through difficulties and discouragements requires men who are more than weaklings.—*The Ministry of Healing*, p. 497.

Instead of thinking of your discouragements, think of the power you can claim in Christ's name. . . . Let your thoughts be directed to the evidences of the great love of God for you. Faith can endure trial, resist temptation, bear up under disappointment. Jesus lives as our advocate. All is ours that His mediation secures. . . . All experiences and circumstances are God's workmen whereby good is brought to us.—*Ibid.*, pp. 488, 489.

When in faith we take hold of His strength, He will change, wonderfully change, the most hopeless, discouraging outlook.—*Testimonies*, vol. 8, p. 12.

Do not dishonor God by words of repining, but praise Him with heart and soul and voice. . . . Do this, and see how smoothly everything will go.—*Selected Messages*, book 2, p. 267.

Some look always at the objectionable and discouraging features, and therefore discouragement overtakes them. They forget that the heavenly universe is waiting to make them agencies of blessing to the world; and that the Lord Jesus is a never-failing storehouse from which human beings may draw strength and courage. There is no need for despondency and apprehension. The time will never come when the shadow of Satan will not be cast athwart our pathway. . . . But our faith should pierce this shadow. God calls for cheerful co-workers, who refuse to become discouraged and disheartened by opposing agencies. The Lord is leading us, and we may go forward courageously, assured that He will be with us, as He was in past years.—*Gospel Workers*, pp. 265, 266.

We are too quickly discouraged, and earnestly cry for the trial to be removed from us, when we should plead for patience to endure and grace to overcome.—*Testimonies*, vol. 1, p. 310.

I have seen the tender love that God has for His people, and it is very great. I saw angels over the saints with their wings spread about them. Each saint had an attending angel. If the saints wept through discouragement, or were in danger, the angels that ever attended them would fly quickly upward to carry the tidings, and the angels in the city would cease to sing. . . . And all the angels in the city would weep. . . . But if the saints fixed their eyes upon the prize before them, and glorified God by praising Him, then the angels would bear the glad tidings to the city, and the angels in the city would touch their golden harps and sing with a loud voice. . . . And the heavenly arches would ring with their lovely songs.—*My Life Today*, p. 302.

Are Your Trials More Than You Can Bear?

The fact that we are called upon to endure trial shows that the Lord Jesus sees in us something precious which He desires to develop. If He saw in us nothing whereby He might glorify His name, He would not spend time in refining us. He does not cast worthless stones into His furnace.—*The Ministry of Healing*, p. 471.

God has a purpose in sending trial to His children. He never leads them otherwise than they would choose to be led if they could see the end from the beginning, and discern the glory of the purpose that they are fulfilling.—*Prophets and Kings*, p. 578.

God's love for His children during the period of their severest trial is as strong and tender as in the days of their sunniest prosperity.—*The Great Controversy*, p. 621.

Seek the Lord for wisdom in every emergency. In every trial plead with Jesus to show you a way out of your troubles, and your eyes will be opened to behold the remedy and to apply to your case the healing promises that have been recorded in His Word. In this way the enemy will find no place to lead you into mourning and unbelief, but instead you will have faith and hope and courage in the Lord. . . . Every draught of bitterness will be mingled with the love of Jesus, and in place of complaining of the bitterness, you will realize that Jesus' love and grace are so mingled with sorrow that it has been turned into subdued, holy, sanctified joy.—*Selected Messages*, book 2, pp. 273, 274.

The precious Saviour will send help just when we need it. The way to heaven is consecrated by His footprints. Every thorn that wounds our feet has wounded His. Every cross that we are called to bear, He has borne before us. The Lord permits conflicts, to prepare the soul for peace.—*Colporteur Ministry*, p. 116.

Our heavenly Father has a thousand ways to provide for us, of which we know nothing. Those who accept the one principle of making the service and honor of God supreme will find perplexities vanish, and a plain path before their feet.—*The Desire of Ages*, p. 330.

Those who are finally victorious will have seasons of terrible perplexity and trial in their religious life; but they must not cast away their confidence, for this is a part of their discipline in the school of Christ, and it is essential in order that all dross may be purged away.—*Messages to Young People*, p. 63.

If received in faith, the trial that seems so bitter and hard to bear will prove a blessing. The cruel blow that blights the joys of earth will be the means of turning our eyes to heaven. How many there are who would never have known Jesus had not sorrow led them to seek comfort in Him!—*Thoughts From the Mount of Blessing*, p. 10.

We need not keep our own record of trials and difficulties, griefs, and sorrows. All these

27

things are written in the books, and heaven will take care of them.—*The Ministry of Healing*, p. 487.

The Saviour is by the side of His tempted and tried ones. With Him there can be no such thing as failure, loss, impossibility, or defeat.—*The Desire of Ages*, p. 490.

Are You Lonely?

We need never feel that we are alone. Angels are our companions. The Comforter that Christ promised to send in His name abides with us. In the way that leads to the City of God there are no difficulties which those who trust in Him may not overcome. There are no dangers which they may not escape. There is not a sorrow, not a grievance, not a human weakness, for which He has not provided a remedy. . . .

He who took humanity upon Himself knows how to sympathize with the sufferings of humanity. Not only does Christ know every soul, and the peculiar needs and trials of that soul, but He knows all the circumstances that chafe and perplex the spirit. His hand is outstretched in pitying tenderness to every

29

suffering child.—*The Ministry of Healing*, p. 249.

Never feel that Christ is far away. He is always near. His loving presence surrounds you.—*Ibid.*, p. 85.

Jesus knows us individually, and is touched with the feeling of our infirmities. He knows us all by name. He knows the very house in which we live, the name of each occupant. He has at times given directions to His servants to go to a certain street in a certain city, to such a house, to find one of His sheep.—*The Desire of Ages*, p. 479.

At all times and in all places, in all sorrows and in all afflictions, when the outlook seems dark and the future perplexing, and we feel helpless and alone, the Comforter will be sent in answer to the prayer of faith.

Circumstances may separate us from every earthly friend; but no circumstance, no distance, can separate us from the heavenly Comforter. Wherever we are, wherever we may go, He is always at our right hand to support, sustain, uphold, and cheer.—*Ibid.*, pp. 669, 670.

We are never alone. Whether we choose Him or not, we have a companion. Remember that wherever you are, whatever you do, God is there.—*The Ministry of Healing,* p. 490.

To those who . . . acquaint themselves with Christ, the earth will nevermore be a lonely and desolate place. It will be their Father's house, filled with the presence of Him who once dwelt among men.—*Education,* p. 120.

God will not suffer one of His truehearted workers to be left alone, to struggle against great odds and be overcome.—*The Ministry of Healing,* p. 488.

Not a sigh is breathed, not a pain felt, not a grief pierces the soul, but the throb vibrates to the Father's heart. . . . God is bending from His throne to hear the cry of the oppressed. To every sincere prayer He answers, "Here am I." He uplifts the distressed and downtrodden. In all our afflictions He is afflicted. In every temptation and every trial the angel of His presence is near to deliver.—*The Desire of Ages,* p. 356.

Every step in life may bring us closer to

Jesus, may give us a deeper experience of His love, and may bring us one step nearer to the blessed home of peace.—*Steps to Christ*, p. 125.

When You Are Tempted

In Christ, God has promised means for subduing every evil trait and resisting every temptation, however strong.—*The Ministry of Healing,* pp. 65, 66.

Jesus revealed no qualities, and exercised no powers, that men may not have through faith in Him. His perfect humanity is that which all His followers may possess, if they will be in subjection to God as He was.—*The Desire of Ages,* p. 664.

Those who fail to realize their constant dependence upon God will be overcome by temptation. We may now suppose that our feet stand secure, and that we shall never be moved.

We may say with confidence, I know in whom I have believed. . . . But Satan is planning to take advantage of our hereditary and cultivated traits of character, and to blind our eyes to our own necessities and defects. Only through realizing our own weakness and looking steadfastly unto Jesus can we walk securely.—*Ibid.,* p. 382.

The Father's presence encircled Christ, and nothing befell Him but that which infinite love permitted for the blessing of the world. Here was His source of comfort, and it is for us. He who is imbued with the Spirit of Christ abides in Christ. The blow that is aimed at him falls upon the Saviour, who surrounds him with His presence. Whatever comes to him comes from Christ. He has no need to resist evil, for Christ is his defense. Nothing can touch him except by our Lord's permission.—*Thoughts From the Mount of Blessing,* p. 71.

Christ will never abandon those for whom He has died. We may leave Him and be overwhelmed with temptation, but Christ can never turn from one for whom He has paid the ransom of His own life.—*Prophets and Kings,* p. 176.

Nothing is apparently more helpless, yet really more invincible, than the soul that feels its nothingness and relies wholly on the merits of the Saviour. God would send every angel in heaven to the aid of such a one, rather than allow him to be overcome.—*Testimonies*, vol. 7, p. 17.

Our heavenly Father measures and weighs every trial before He permits it to come upon the believer. He considers the circumstances and the strength of the one who is to stand under the proving and test of God, and He never permits the temptations to be greater than the capacity of resistance. If the soul is overborne, the person overpowered, this can never be charged to God, as failing to give strength in grace, but the one tempted was not vigilant and prayerful and did not appropriate by faith the provisions God had abundantly in store for him. Christ never failed a believer in his hour of combat. The believer must claim the promise and meet the foe in the name of the Lord, and he will not know anything like failure.—Ellen G. White manuscript 6, 1889.

Could our spiritual vision be quickened, we should see souls bowed under oppression and burdened with grief. . . . We should see angels flying quickly to the aid of these tempted ones, forcing back the hosts of evil that encompass them, and placing their feet on the sure foundation.—*Prophets and Kings*, p. 176.

If You've Sinned

The love of God still yearns over the one who has chosen to separate from Him, and He sets in operation influences to bring him back to the Father's house. . . . A golden chain, the mercy and compassion of divine love, is passed around every imperiled soul.—*Christ's Object Lessons*, p. 202.

We should ever bear in mind that we are all erring mortals, and that Christ exercises much pity for our weakness, and loves us although we err.—*Testimonies*, vol. 1, p. 383.

We shall often have to bow down and weep at the feet of Jesus because of our shortcomings and mistakes, but we are not to be discouraged. . . . We are not cast off, not forsaken and rejected of God.—*Steps to Christ,* p. 64.

By prayer, by the study of His word, by faith in His abiding presence, the weakest of human beings may live in contact with the living Christ, and He will hold them by a hand that will never let go.—*The Ministry of Healing,* p. 182.

So long as we do not consent to sin, there is no power, whether human or satanic, that can bring a stain upon the soul.—*Thoughts From the Mount of Blessing,* p. 32.

The only defense against evil is the indwelling of Christ in the heart through faith in His righteousness. . . . We may leave off many bad habits, for the time we may part company with Satan; but without a vital connection with God, through the surrender of ourselves to Him moment by moment, we shall be overcome. Without a personal acquaintance with Christ, and a continual communion, we are at the mercy of the enemy, and shall do his bidding in the end.—*The Desire of Ages,* p. 324.

If one who daily communes with God errs

from the path, if he turns a moment from looking steadfastly unto Jesus, it is not because he sins wilfully; for when he sees his mistake, he turns again, and fastens his eyes upon Jesus, and the fact that he has erred, does not make him less dear to the heart of God.—Ellen G. White, in *Review and Herald,* May 12, 1896.

If in our ignorance we make missteps, Christ does not leave us.—*Christ's Object Lessons,* p. 173.

Christ is ready to set us free from sin, but He does not force the will; and if by persistent transgression the will itself is wholly bent on evil, and we do not *desire* to be set free, if we *will* not accept His grace, what more can He do? We have destroyed ourselves by our determined rejection of His love.—*Steps to Christ,* p. 34.

Many, walking along the path of life, dwell upon their mistakes and failures and disappointments, and their hearts are filled with grief and discouragement. . . . It is not wise to gather together all the unpleasant recollections of a past life—its iniquities and disappointments— to talk over them and mourn over them until we are overwhelmed with discouragement. A discouraged soul is filled with darkness, shutting out the light of God from his own soul and casting a shadow upon the pathway of others.—*Ibid.*, pp. 116, 117.

Do You Feel Like an Outcast?

None have fallen so low, none are so vile, but that they can find deliverance in Christ. . . . No cry from a soul in need, though it fail of utterance in words, will be unheeded. Those who will consent to enter into covenant relation with the God of heaven are not left to the power of Satan or to the infirmity of their own nature.—*The Desire of Ages*, pp. 258, 259.

Do not listen to the enemy's suggestion to stay away from Christ until you have made yourself better, until you are good enough to come to God. If you wait until then you will never come. When Satan points to your filthy garments, repeat the promise of the Saviour, "Him that cometh to me I will in no wise cast out." John 6:37.—*Prophets and Kings*, p. 320.

The relations between God and each soul are as distinct and full as though there were not another soul upon the earth to share His watchcare, not another soul for whom He gave His beloved Son.—*Steps to Christ*, p. 100.

Every Christian must stand on guard continually, watching every avenue of the soul where Satan might find access. He must pray for divine help and at the same time resolutely resist every inclination to sin.—*Testimonies*, vol. 5, p. 47.

By choosing to sin, men separate themselves from God, cut themselves off from the channel of blessing, and the sure result is ruin and death.—*Selected Messages*, book 1, p. 235.

His [the Saviour's] heart of divine love and sympathy is drawn out most of all for the one who is the most hopelessly entangled in the snares of the enemy.—*The Ministry of Healing*, pp. 89, 90.

God does not give us up because of our sins.

42

We may make mistakes, and grieve His Spirit; but when we repent, and come to Him with contrite hearts, He will not turn us away.— *Ibid.*, p. 350.

As the shepherd loves his sheep, and cannot rest if even one be missing, so, in an infinitely higher degree, does God love every outcast soul. Men may deny the claim of His love, they may wander from Him, they may choose another master; yet they are God's, and He longs to recover His own.—*Christ's Object Lessons*, p. 187.

Whatever may have been your past experience, however discouraging your present circumstances, if you will come to Jesus just as you are, weak, helpless, and despairing, our compassionate Saviour will meet you a great way off, and will throw about you His arms of love and His robe of righteousness.—*Thoughts From the Mount of Blessing*, p. 9.

When Sickness Comes

The prayer that comes from an earnest heart, when the simple wants of the soul are expressed, as we would ask an earthly friend for a favor, expecting it to be granted—this is the prayer of faith. God does not desire our ceremonial compliments, but the unspoken cry of the heart broken and subdued with a sense of its sin and utter weakness finds its way to the Father of all mercy.—*Ibid.*, pp. 86, 87.

To those who desire prayer for their restoration to health, it should be made plain that the violation of God's law, either natural or spiritual, is sin, and that in order for them to receive His blessing, sin must be confessed and forsaken.—*The Ministry of Healing*, p. 228.

44

Often those who are in health forget the wonderful mercies continued to them day by day, year after year, and they render no tribute of praise to God for His benefits. But when sickness comes, God is remembered. When human strength fails, men feel their need of divine help. And never does our merciful God turn from the soul that in sincerity seeks Him for help. He is our refuge in sickness as in health.—*Ibid.*, p. 225.

I saw that if we do not feel immediate answers to our prayers, we should hold fast our faith, not allowing distrust to come in, for that will separate us from God. . . . Our confidence in God should be strong; and when we need it most, the blessing will fall upon us like a shower of rain.—*Testimonies,* vol. 1, p. 121.

The same power that Christ exercised when He walked visibly among men is in His word. It was by His word that Jesus healed disease and cast out demons. . . . So with all the promises of God's word. In them He is speaking to us individually, speaking as directly as if we could listen to His voice. It is in these promises that Christ communicates to us His grace and power.—*The Ministry of Healing,* p. 122.

45

Our Lord has given us definite instruction, through the apostle James, as to our duty in case of sickness. When human help fails, God will be the helper of His people. "Is any sick among you? let him call for the elders of the church; and let them pray over him, anointing him with oil in the name of the Lord: and the prayer of faith shall save the sick, and the Lord shall raise him up."—*Counsels on Health*, p. 457.

Sometimes answers to our prayers come immediately; sometimes we have to wait patiently and continue earnestly to plead for the things that we need. . . . There are precious promises in the Scriptures to those who wait upon the Lord. We all desire an immediate answer to our prayers, and are tempted to become discouraged if our prayer is not immediately answered. . . . The delay is for our special benefit.—*Ibid.*, pp. 380, 381.

If you will find voice and time to pray, God will find time and voice to answer.—*My Life Today*, p. 16.

46

When Death Comes

Let the peace of Christ come into your soul. Be true in your trust because He is true to His promise. Lay your poor, nervous hand in His firm hand and let Him hold you and strengthen you, cheer and comfort you.—*Selected Messages*, book 2, p. 254.

God would not have us remain pressed down by dumb sorrow, with sore and breaking hearts. He would have us look up and behold His dear face of love. The blessed Saviour stands by many whose eyes are so blinded by tears that they do not discern Him. He longs to clasp our hands, to have us look to Him in simple faith, permitting Him to guide us. His heart is open to our griefs, our sorrows, and our

47

trials. . . . He will lift the soul above the daily sorrow and perplexity, into a realm of peace.— *Thoughts From the Mount of Blessing,* p. 12.

If with a humble heart you seek divine guidance in every trouble and perplexity, His word is pledged that a gracious answer will be given you.—*Testimonies,* vol. 5, p. 427.

In the darkest days, when appearances seem most forbidding, fear not. Have faith in God. He knows your need. He has all power. His infinite love and compassion never weary. Fear not that He will fail of fulfilling His promise. He is eternal truth. Never will He change the covenant He has made with those who love Him. And He will bestow upon His faithful servants the measure of efficiency that their need demands.—*Prophets and Kings,* pp. 164, 165.

When in trouble, many think they must appeal to some earthly friend, telling him their perplexities, and begging for help. Under trying circumstances unbelief fills their hearts, and the way seems dark. And all the time there stands beside them the mighty Counselor of the ages, inviting them to place their confidence in

Him. Jesus, the great Burden Bearer, is saying, "Come unto me, . . . and I will give you rest." Shall we turn from Him to uncertain human beings, who are as dependent upon God as we ourselves are?—*The Ministry of Healing*, p. 512.

Those who have borne the greatest sorrows are frequently the ones who carry the greatest comfort to others, bringing sunshine wherever they go. Such ones have been chastened and sweetened by their afflictions; they did not lose confidence in God when trouble assailed them, but clung closer to His protecting love. Such ones are a living proof of the tender care of God, who makes the darkness as well as the light, and chastens us for our good.—*Selected Messages*, book 2, p. 274.

We have a living, risen Saviour. . . . The Life-giver is soon to come. . . . He is to bring forth the captives and proclaim, "I am the resurrection and the life." There stands the risen host. The last thought was of death and its pangs. . . . But now they proclaim, "O death, where is thy sting? O grave, where is thy victory?" . . .

Here they stand, and the finishing touch of

49

immortality is put upon them, and they go up to meet their Lord in the air. The gates of the city of God swing back upon their hinges, and the nations that have kept the truth enter in.—*The Seventh-day Adventist Bible Commentary*, Ellen G. White Comments, on 1 Cor. 15:51-55, p. 1093.

Go right forward as if every prayer offered was lodged in the throne of God and responded to by the One whose promises never fail. Go right along, singing and making melody to God in your hearts, even when depressed by a sense of weight and sadness. . . . Light will come, joy will be ours, and the mists and clouds will be rolled back.—*Selected Messages*, book 2, pp. 242, 243.

Do You Need Guidance?

So long as we surrender the will to God, and trust in His strength and wisdom, we shall be guided in safe paths, to fulfill our appointed part in His great plan.—*The Desire of Ages*, p. 209.

Those who decide to do nothing in any line that will displease God, will know, after presenting their case before him, just what course to pursue. And they will receive not only wisdom, but strength.—*Ibid.*, p. 668.

Our fondest hopes are often blighted here. Our loved ones are torn from us by death. . . . But hope bears our spirits up. We are not parted forever, but shall meet the loved ones who sleep in Jesus. They shall come again from the land of the enemy. The Life-giver is coming. Myriads of holy angels escort Him on His way. He bursts the bands of death, breaks the fetters of the tomb, the precious captives come forth in health and immortal beauty.—*Selected Messages*, book 2, pp. 259, 260.

As we commit ourselves to the wise Master Worker, He will bring out the pattern of life and character that will be to His own glory.—*The Desire of Ages*, p. 331.

We are to exercise wisdom and judgment in every action of life, that we may not, by reckless movements, place ourselves in trial. We are not to plunge into difficulties, neglecting the means God has provided, and misusing the faculties He has given us. Christ's workers are to obey His instructions implicitly. The work is God's, and if we would bless others His plans must be followed. Self cannot be made a center; self can receive no honor. If we plan according to our own ideas, the Lord will leave us to our own mistakes. But when, after following His directions, we are brought into strait places, He will deliver us.—*Ibid.*, p. 369.

We have not wisdom to plan our own lives.

It is not for us to shape our future. . . . We [should] depend upon God, that our lives may be the simple outworking of His will. As we commit our ways to Him, He will direct our steps.—*The Ministry of Healing*, pp. 478, 479.

If we surrender our lives to His service, we can never be placed in a position for which God has not made provision. Whatever may be our situation, we have a Guide to direct our way; whatever our perplexities, we have a sure Counselor; whatever our sorrow, bereavement, or loneliness, we have a sympathizing Friend. If in our ignorance we make missteps, Christ does not leave us. His voice, clear and distinct, is heard saying, "I am the way, the truth, and the life."—*Christ's Object Lessons*, p. 173.

In His loving care and interest for us, often He who understands us better than we understand ourselves refuses to permit us selfishly to seek the gratification of our own ambition. He does not permit us to pass by the homely but sacred duties that lie next us. Often these duties afford the very training essential to prepare us for a higher work. Often our plans fail that God's plans for us may succeed.—*The Ministry of Healing*, p. 473.

If you will seek the Lord and be converted every day; if you will of your own spiritual choice be free and joyous in God; if with gladsome consent of heart to His gracious call you come wearing the yoke of Christ—the yoke of obedience and service—all your murmurings will be stilled, all your difficulties will be removed, all the perplexing problems that now confront you will be solved.—*Thoughts From the Mount of Blessing,* p. 101.

We need to follow more closely God's plan of life. To do our best in the work that lies nearest, to commit our ways to God, and to watch for the indications of His providence—these are rules that ensure safe guidance in the choice of an occupation.—*Education,* p. 267.

Have You Been Falsely Accused?

The Lord is able to render futile every agency that works for the defeat of His chosen ones.—*Prophets and Kings*, p. 487.

Let not the unkind speeches of men hurt you. Did not men say unkind things about Jesus? You err, and may sometimes give occasion for unkind remarks; but Jesus never did. He was pure, spotless, undefiled. . . . It may be that even the members of the church to which you belong will say and do that which will grieve you. But move right on, calm and peaceful, ever trusting in Jesus, remembering that you are not your own, that you are Christ's property, the purchase of the blood of God's beloved Son, and that you are engaged in His work, seeking to bless humanity.—*Testimonies*, vol. 8, p. 129.

While slander may blacken the reputation, it cannot stain the character. That is in God's keeping. So long as we do not consent to sin, there is no power, whether human or satanic, that can bring a stain upon the soul. A man whose heart is stayed upon God is just the same in the hour of his most afflicting trials and most discouraging surroundings as when he was in prosperity, when the light and favor of God seemed to be upon him.—*Thoughts From the Mount of Blessing*, p. 32.

Christ has given us His life as a pattern, and we dishonor Him when we become jealous of every slight, and are ready to resent every injury, supposed or real. It is not an evidence of a noble mind to be prepared to defend self, to preserve our own dignity. We would better suffer wrongfully a hundred times than wound the soul by a spirit of retaliation, or by giving vent to wrath. There is strength to be obtained of God. He can help. He can give grace and heavenly wisdom. If you ask in faith, you will receive; but you must watch unto prayer.—*Testimonies*, vol. 2, pp. 426, 427.

If you are ill-treated or wrongfully accused, instead of returning an angry answer, repeat to yourself the precious promises.—*The Ministry of Healing,* p. 486.

It does not behoove those from whom Jesus has so much to bear, in their failings and perversity, to be ever mindful of slights and real or imaginary offense. And yet there are those who are ever suspecting the motives of others about them. They see offense and slights where no such thing was intended. All this is Satan's work.—Ellen G. White manuscript 24, 1887.

We may expect that false reports will circulate about us; but if we follow a straight course, if we remain indifferent to these things, others will also be indifferent. Let us leave to God the care of our reputation. . . . Slander can be lived down by our manner of living; it is not lived down by words of indignation. Let our great anxiety be to act in the fear of God, and show by our conduct that these reports are false. No one can injure our character as much as ourselves.—*Ibid.*

So long as we are in the world, we shall meet with adverse influences. There will be provocations to test the temper; and it is by meeting these in a right spirit that the Christian graces are developed. If Christ dwells in us, we shall be patient, kind, and forbearing, cheerful amid frets and irritations.—*The Ministry of Healing,* p. 487.

To be silent is the strongest rebuke that you can give to one who is speaking harsh, discourteous words to you. Keep perfectly silent. Often silence is eloquence.—*Child Guidance,* p. 551.

If a Friend Fails You

God will be nearer and dearer to you than any of your earthly relatives can be. He will be your friend and will never leave you. . . . His friendship will prove sweet peace to you.— *Testimonies*, vol. 2, p. 314.

Of all persecution the hardest to bear is variance in the home, the estrangement of dearest earthly friends. But Jesus declares, "He that loveth father or mother more than me is not worthy of me."—*The Desire of Ages*, p. 357.

There are many living martyrs today who suffer in silence, who trust in God when they are abused with the tongue and who are

59

tantalized, who are hurt and wounded by coarse, harsh denunciations, whose lot seems to be to live and to suffer, receiving comfort only from Jesus who is the Source of their strength. Such souls are missionaries. They are Christ's noble ones, and their names are written in the Lamb's Book of Life.—Ellen G. White manuscript 9, 1868.

In one moment, by the hasty, passionate, careless tongue, may be wrought evil that a whole life time's repentance cannot undo. Oh, the hearts that are broken, the friends estranged, the lives wrecked, by the harsh, hasty words of those who might have brought help and healing!—*Education,* pp. 236, 237.

Until the judgment you will never know the influence of a kind, considerate course toward the inconsistent, the unreasonable, the unworthy. When we meet with ingratitude and betrayal of sacred trusts, we are roused to show our contempt or indignation. This the guilty expect; they are prepared for it. But kind forbearance takes them by surprise and often awakens their better impulses and arouses a longing for a nobler life.—*The Ministry of Healing,* p. 495.

In His mercy and faithfulness God often permits those in whom we place confidence to fail us, in order that we may learn the folly of trusting in man. . . . Let us trust fully, humbly, unselfishly in God.—*Ibid.*, p. 486.

Of all the gifts that heaven can bestow upon men, fellowship with Christ in His sufferings is the most weighty trust and the highest honor.—*Ibid.*, p. 478.

Remember, Jesus knows it all—every sorrow, every grief—He will not leave you to sink, for His arms are beneath you. You may be an enlightenment to a whole neighborhood if you are indeed patient, kind, forbearing.—Ellen G. White manuscript 9, 1868.

Have You Lost Your Faith?

The Lord would have all His sons and daughters happy, peaceful, and obedient. Through the exercise of faith the believer comes into possession of these blessings. Through faith, every deficiency of character may be supplied, every defilement cleansed, every fault corrected, every excellence developed.—*The Acts of the Apostles*, p. 564.

All your happiness, peace, joy, and success in this life are dependent upon genuine, trusting faith in God.—*Messages to Young People*, p. 410.

It is faith that connects us with heaven, and brings us strength for coping with the powers of darkness. In Christ, God has provided means for subduing every sinful trait, and resisting every temptation, however strong. But many feel that they lack faith, and therefore they remain away from Christ. Let these souls, in their helpless unworthiness, cast themselves upon the mercy of their compassionate Saviour. Look not to self, but to Christ. He who healed the sick and cast out demons when He walked among men is the same mighty Redeemer today. Faith comes by the word of God.—*The Desire of Ages*, p. 429.

Faith looks beyond the difficulties, and lays hold of the unseen, even Omnipotence, therefore it cannot be baffled. Faith is the clasping of the hand of Christ in every emergency.—*Gospel Workers*, p. 262.

Nothing more quickly inspires faith than the exercise of faith.—*Prophets and Kings*, p. 351.

Faith is trusting God—believing that He loves us and knows best what is for our good. Thus, instead of our own, it leads us to choose His way. In place of our ignorance, it accepts His wisdom; in place of our weakness, His strength; in place of our sinfulness, His righteousness.—*Education*, p. 253.

Faith is the living power that presses through every barrier, overrides all obstacles, and plants its banner in the heart of the enemy's camp. God will do marvelous things for those who trust in Him.—*Testimonies*, vol. 4, p. 163.

God never asks us to believe, without giving sufficient evidence upon which to base our faith. His existence, His character, the truthfulness of His word, are all established by testimony that appeals to our reason; and this testimony is abundant. Yet God has never removed the possibility of doubt. Our faith must rest upon evidence, not demonstration. Those who wish to doubt will have opportunity; while those who really desire to know the truth will find plenty of evidence on which to rest their faith.—*Steps to Christ*, p. 105.

The faith of him who is constantly advancing does not weaken; for above, beneath, beyond, he recognizes Infinite Love, working out all things to accomplish His good purpose.—*Prophets and Kings*, p. 660.